SO-AAC-278

**HEINEMANN STATE STUDIES**

# Uniquely
# Maryland

Jennifer Leese

**Heinemann Library**
Chicago, Illinois

© 2004 Heinemann Library
a division of Reed Elsevier Inc.
Chicago, Illinois

Customer Service    888-454-2279

Visit our website at www.heinemannlibrary.com

All rights reserved. No part of this publication
may be reproduced or transmitted in any form or
by any means, electronic or mechanical, including
photocopying, recording, taping, or any
information storage and retrieval system, without
permission in writing from the publisher.

Designed by Heinemann Library
Printed in China by WKT Company Limited.

08  07  06  05  04
10  9  8  7  6  5  4  3  2  1

**Library of Congress
Cataloging-in-Publication Data**

Leese, Jennifer, 1970–
  Uniquely Maryland / Jennifer Leese.
     p. cm.—(State studies)
Summary: Provides an overview of various aspects
of Maryland that make it a unique state, including
its people, land, government, culture, economy,
and attractions.
Includes bibliographical references and index.
  ISBN 1-4034-4493-5 — ISBN 1-4034-4508-7 (pbk.)
  1. Maryland—Juvenile literature. [1. Maryland.]
I. Title. II. Series.
  F181.3.L44 2003
  975.2—dc21

                                        2003008980

**Cover Pictures**

**Top** (left to right) Crabs from the Chesa-
peake Bay, Maryland state flag, Edgar Allan
Poe, Camden Yards Ballpark **Main** Naval
Academy in Annapolis

**Acknowledgments**
Development and photo research by
BOOK BUILDERS LLC

The author and publishers are grateful to the fol-
lowing for permission to reproduce copyrighted
material:

Cover photographs by (top, L-R): Paul A. Souders/
Corbis; Joseph Sohm/ChromoSohm Inc/
Corbis; Bettmann/Corbis; Joseph Sohm/
ChromoSohm/Corbis; (Main) Kevin Fleming/Corbis.

Title page (L-R) Gilbert S. Grant/Photo Researchers.
Chuck Pefley/Alamy; Andre Jenny/Alamy. Contents
page: Maryland Office of Tourism Development;
p. 4 Courtesy Jeffery Howe; p. 5, 6 Cameron
Davidson/Getty Images; p. 8 Paul A. Sanders/
Corbis; p. 8, 43, 45 maps by IMA for Book Builders
LLC; p. 10 Omikron/Photo Researchers; p. 11
Hulton/Getty Images; pp. 12T, 38 Joseph Sohm;
ChromoSohm Inc/Corbis; pp. 12B, 20, 37, 40
HistoricGraphics.com/Ross J. Kelbaugh Collection;
pp. 13, 15T, 19, 23, 35 Maryland Office of Tourism
Development; p. 15M Lawrence Naylor/Photo
Researchers; p. 15B Tim Davis/Photo Researchers;
p. 16T Maria Zom/AnimalsAnimals; p. 16M Daniel
Teetor/Alamy; p. 16B Gilbert S. Grant/Photo
Researchers; p. 17T Carmela Leszczynski/Animals
Animals; p. 17M Courtesy R.A.R.E. Photographic;
p. 18 George Monserrate Schwartz/Alamy; p. 21
Smithsonian; p. 24 Bettman/Corbis; p. 25B
HistoricGraphics.com/Library of Congress; p. 26,
30, 42 Andre Jenny/Alamy; p. 27 Paul A. Souders/
Corbis; p. 28 Tom Darden; p. 32 Kevin Fleming/
Corbis; p. 33 Courtesy Baltimore Area Convention
and Visitors Association; p. 36 R. Capozzelli/
Heinemann Library; p. 39 Courtesy Maryland
Media Relations. p. 41 Chuck Pefley/Alamy; p. 43
Courtesy The Great Blacks in Wax Museum; p. 44
Courtesy Chesapeake Bay Maritime Museum.

Special thanks to Jessica Elfenbein of the University
of Baltimore for her expert comments in the prepa-
ration of this book.

Every effort has been made to contact copyright
holders of any material reproduced in this book.
Any omissions will be rectified in subsequent
printings if notice is given to the publisher.

Some words are shown in bold, **like this.**
You can find out what they mean by looking
in the glossary.

# Contents

# Uniquely Maryland

**W**hen people call something unique, they mean that nothing else is exactly like it.

The state of Maryland is unique. Maryland ranks 42nd in size among the states, yet it includes so many different features. Maryland is home to the country's first **cathedral,** finished in 1821. The legendary Babe Ruth was born in Maryland, and Francis Scott Key wrote the national anthem on a boat in Baltimore Harbor. These are just a few examples of the unique and interesting things about Maryland.

## ORIGIN OF THE STATE'S NAME

In 1632 the English King Charles I granted land in the American colonies to the Calverts, a wealthy English family. The king wanted only two things in return. He asked that the Calverts send him two arrowheads each year, and that the new colony's name honor the king's wife, Queen Henrietta Maria, known as Mary.

*Basilica of the Assumption of the Blessed Virgin Mary.*

*Annapolis was settled in 1649. Originally called Providence, it was later known as Anne Arundel Town, after the wife of Lord Baltimore. In 1695 it became the capital of Maryland and was renamed Annapolis for Princess Anne, who later became queen of England*

## MAJOR CITIES

Annapolis, 25 miles south of Baltimore, where the Severn River meets the Chesapeake Bay, is Maryland's capital. This **colonial**-era city is home to the U.S. Naval Academy, which was established in 1845. So many boats can be found in Annapolis that people refer to the city as the "sailing capital of the United States."

Baltimore, the largest city in Maryland, is in the central part of the state, where the Patapsco River empties into the Chesapeake Bay. Founded in 1729, Baltimore offered a natural, deep-water harbor farther west than other Atlantic ports. It became a bustling departure point for trade and travel to the western parts of the country. The city grew quickly as **immigrants** built a series of ethnic neighborhoods beyond the harbor. Today, Baltimore attracts more than fifteen million visitors each year. Many go to the scenic waterfront area known as the Inner Harbor, which includes the Maryland Science Center and the National Aquarium.

Columbia, located about fifteen miles southwest of Baltimore, was one of the first **planned communities** in the United States. In the early 1960s, a man named James W. Rouse decided to build a new city. He planned a community for people of all races, religions, and backgrounds. Rouse achieved his goal. Today, more than 90,000 people live in Columbia.

# Maryland's Geography and Climate

**M**aryland lies on the eastern coast of the United States. Its northern border with Pennsylvania follows the **Mason–Dixon Line.** Delaware and the Atlantic Ocean are to the east of Maryland. West Virginia, Virginia, and Washington, D.C., are to the west and south.

## REGIONS

Three main land regions cover Maryland. The Appalachian Ridge and Valley, the Piedmont Plateau, and the Atlantic Coastal Plain stretch from west to east. The Appalachian Ridge and Valley section, known as western Maryland, includes the state's highest point, Backbone Mountain, at 3,360 feet.

From the mountainous western area, the Piedmont Plateau region gently descends from the Appalachian region in a series of rolling hills. Farms dot Maryland's

*The Chesapeake Bay divides Maryland into two parts, the Eastern Shore and the Western Shore.*

section of the Piedmont Plateau, which extends from New York to Alabama.

The Atlantic Coastal Plain meets the Piedmont Plateau at the fall line, where rivers fall toward the plain. Maryland's largest land region, the Atlantic Coastal Plain covers more than half the state. This low-lying area of sandy soils and marshes surrounds the Chesapeake Bay and extends to the Atlantic Ocean.

## CLIMATE AND PRECIPITATION

Maryland has a **temperate** climate. Summer temperatures vary from mild to hot, and winter temperatures are extremely cold only in the mountains of western Maryland. In Baltimore, the normal low temperature for January is 29° F, and the normal high temperature for July is 91° F. Western Maryland, with its higher elevation and greater distance from the Atlantic, is cooler, with a normal January low of 17° F and a normal July high of 79° F.

The Gulf Stream, a warm water current, flows north through the Atlantic Ocean from the Gulf of Mexico. As it passes the Maryland coastline, the Gulf Stream helps raise

# Saving an Eastern Shore Ecosystem

Blackwater National Wildlife Refuge, established in 1933, seeks to preserve the **ecosystem** unique to Maryland's Eastern Shore. More than 25,000 acres of marshlands, ponds, forests, and fields harbor nearly 400 species of wildlife, including numerous bald eagles. Blackwater also has the world's largest protected population of the **endangered** Delmarva fox squirrel, a large gray squirrel whose **habitat** shrank as the area's human population grew. Visitors to the refuge can follow walking and driving trails to view the ecosystem up close.

*Storms gain power while over the open ocean, leaving coastal areas in danger. In 1933 a strong storm changed the layout of Ocean City by cutting a new channel through town lands into the bay behind it.*

temperatures in the eastern part of the state. The Atlantic also brings powerful storms to Maryland's shores.

Maryland's weather is neither especially dry nor especially wet. The average annual rainfall is about 41 inches. Rainfall peaks in July and August when thunderstorms hit the area about once every five days. During the winter, snowfall varies by region. Garrett County, in the mountainous western region, averages more than 100 inches per year. At the other end of the state, on the lower Eastern Shore, snowfall averages about ten inches per year.

## Average Annual Precipitation in Maryland

*In Maryland, the most precipitation falls on the mountains in the western part of the state. As air rises to cross the mountains, it cools. As the air cools, clouds form, making precipitation more likely.*

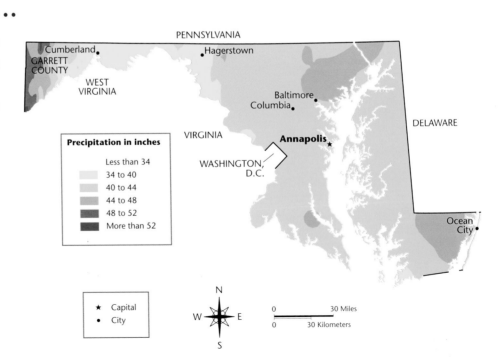

# Famous Firsts

## FIRST CATHOLIC BISHOP IN THE UNITED STATES

Born in Upper Marlboro, Maryland, John Carroll (1735–1815) attended school in France, taught at **Catholic** schools there, and became a priest. In 1789, Pope Pius VI named John Carroll **bishop** of Baltimore, the first Roman Catholic bishop in the United States. That same year Carroll founded a Catholic college, known today as Georgetown University.

## FIRST MONUMENT TO COLUMBUS IN THE WESTERN HEMISPHERE

In 1792 a Frenchman living in Baltimore was shocked to learn that the Americas had no monument to Christopher Columbus. Charles Francois Adrien Le Paulmier built a 44-foot-tall, brick-and-cement obelisk, or four-sided pillar, on his property. Paulmier dedicated the monument on the 300th anniversary of Columbus's first voyage to the continent.

## REFRIGERATOR INVENTED

In 1803 Thomas Moore, an engineer from Maryland, invented the first refrigerator. Moore was looking for a way to carry butter from farms in Maryland to Washington, D.C. He lined a cedar tub with sheet metal and padded it with rabbit fur. Then he filled the container with ice to keep the butter from melting. It worked!

## WORLD'S FIRST DENTAL COLLEGE

In 1840 two Maryland dentists, Horace H. Hayden (1769–1844) and Chapin A. Harris (1806–1860), founded the first dental college in the world—the Baltimore

## Tom Thumb Versus a Horse

In 1830 Peter Cooper had built a steam locomotive called *Tom Thumb*. But *Tom Thumb* had no work, because the Baltimore and Ohio Railroad—which depended on horses to pull the trains—was not convinced that steam power would work better. The railroad agreed to give Cooper a chance to prove his claims, and they set up a race. The contest did not go the way Cooper had hoped. The engine belt on *Tom Thumb* slipped, and the horse won. They tried again. This time, *Tom Thumb* won the race. The Baltimore and Ohio Railroad was convinced, and train travel would never be the same.

College of Dental Surgery. Students there learned science, general medicine, and specialized dental skills. Dental colleges founded in later years modeled themselves after the one in Baltimore. Today, the Baltimore College of Dental Surgery is part of the University of Maryland.

### First Public High School for Girls

In 1844 the Eastern Female High School opened as the first public high school for girls. The building that housed the school beginning in 1870 still stands at the corner of Aisquith and Orleans streets in Baltimore.

## FIRST TELEGRAPH LINE

On May 24, 1844, the message "What hath God wrought" traveled over the first **electromagnetic** telegraph line. That line, held high on wooden poles, ran between Baltimore and Washington, D.C. Samuel Morse, who sat at one end of the line, invented the code used for the message. In Morse code, long and short sounds stand for the letters of the alphabet. The invention of the telegraph, along with Morse code, let people communicate quickly over long distances. For the first time, news of events happening far away could be known almost immediately.

## FIRST ICE CREAM FACTORY

In 1851 Baltimore dairy farmer Jacob Fussell started the first ice cream factory in the United States. As a way to use up extra cream from his dairy, he began making vanilla ice cream with a large hand-cranked machine. Fussell sold his ice cream for 60¢ a quart.

*Florence Sabin taught school for three years to earn enough money to go to Johns Hopkins Medical School, which she entered in 1896.*

## FIRST WOMAN PROFESSOR AT A MEDICAL SCHOOL

Florence Sabin (1871–1953), the first woman to graduate from Johns Hopkins University Medical School, became a professor there in 1917. She was the first woman professor at a U.S. medical school. Sabin was also the first female member of the National Academy of Sciences, which honors those who have made important contributions to science.

# Maryland's State Symbols

*Marylanders must be careful when they fly the state flag. The design makes it hard to tell if the flag is upside down. To fly it correctly, the black part of the black and gold design must be in the corner at the top of the flagpole.*

### MARYLAND STATE FLAG

Maryland's flag is the only **heraldic banner** among the state flags, displaying the **coats of arms** of two English families. The black and gold design represents the Calvert family, the founders of Maryland. George Calvert's mother was a Crossland, and the red and white cross represents her side of the family.

### MARYLAND STATE SEAL

The governor and secretary of state **emboss** official documents with the Great Seal of Maryland. The reverse side of the seal (the one usually seen) shows the

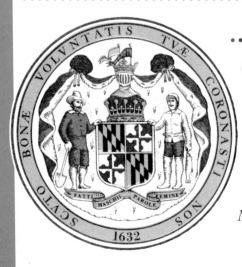

*The Calvert family motto, on a yellow scroll, reads* Fatti maschii parole femine. *That is Italian for "strong deeds, gentle words." The Latin around the rim reads, "With favor wilt thou compass us as with a shield." The date on the seal—1632—refers to the year that Charles I granted Maryland's charter.*

Calvert and Crossland coats of arms on a shield. A gold crown and a knight's helmet rest above the shield, and a farmer and a fisherman stand to either side. The crown and helmet suggest power, and the men symbolize **Lord Baltimore**'s two estates—the one in Maryland and another in Newfoundland.

The other side of the seal shows Cecil Calvert on a horse draped with the colors of the Calvert and Crossland families. The Latin words around the rim mean "Cecil, Absolute Lord of Maryland and Avalon, Baron of Baltimore."

## STATE NICKNAME: THE OLD LINE STATE

Maryland's nickname, "The Old Line State," came about during the **Revolutionary War** (1775–1783). No one knows exactly how it happened. In one version of the story, 400 soldiers from Maryland held a line of defense against a British force of 10,000. Their bravery impressed General George Washington, who praised "the old line" for helping his troops escape danger.

## STATE FLOWER: BLACK-EYED SUSAN

In 1896 a group of women meeting at the Maryland **Agricultural** College decided that Maryland needed a state flower. They chose the black-eyed Susan because the flowers grow all over the state, and their black centers and gold petals match the state colors. In 1918 the General Assembly voted it the official "Floral Emblem" of Maryland.

*Black-eyed Susans bloom in late summer. They often grow along the sides of country roads.*

# "Maryland! My Maryland!"

The despot's heel is on thy shore,
Maryland! My Maryland!
His torch is at thy temple door,
Maryland! My Maryland!
Avenge the patriotic gore
That flecked the streets of Baltimore,
And be the battle queen of yore,
Maryland! My Maryland!

Hark to an exiled son's appeal,
Maryland! My Maryland!
My mother State! to thee I kneel,
Maryland! My Maryland!
For life and death, for woe and weal,

Thy peerless chivalry reveal,
And gird thy beauteous limbs with
    steel,
Maryland! My Maryland!

Thou wilt not cower in the dust,
Maryland! My Maryland!
Thy beaming sword shall never rust,
Maryland! My Maryland!
Remember Carroll's sacred trust,
Remember Howard's warlike thrust,
And all thy slumberers with the just,
Maryland! My Maryland!

## STATE SONG: "MARYLAND! MY MARYLAND!"

Marylander James Ryder Randall wrote the nine-stanza poem "Maryland! My Maryland!" in 1861, and sisters Jennie and Hetty Cary of Baltimore suggested singing Randall's poem to the tune of "Oh, Christmas Tree." "Maryland! My Maryland!" became the official state song in 1939.

## STATE TREE: WHITE OAK

The white oak has been Maryland's state tree since 1941. That year Maryland bought a famous Maryland land-mark, the Wye Oak. This magnificent, 96-foot white oak stood at Wye Mills on the Eastern Shore. White oaks more than 50 years old may drop up to 10,000 acorns each year. Native Americans ground those acorns into flour, a practice they shared with European settlers.

④

*Maryland's state bird, the Baltimore oriole, also known as the northern oriole, has been a protected species since 1882.*

## STATE BIRD: BALTIMORE ORIOLE

Maryland's state bird is the Baltimore oriole. The male bird's black and gold feathers match the Calvert family colors. Some say that Cecil Calvert, Lord Baltimore, saw a flock of orioles and noticed their coloring himself. The birds soon became known by the Baltimore name. Today, the Baltimore oriole rarely appears in Maryland. Its **habitat** has shrunk, and **insecticides** have poisoned the birds along with the insects they eat.

## STATE FISH: ROCKFISH

In 1965 the Maryland General Assembly chose the rockfish as the state fish because of its fighting ability and tasty meat. The rockfish may live as long as 30 years.

*Also known as the striped bass, the rockfish has silvery coloring with seven or eight dark stripes along its sides. The biggest rockfish caught in the Chesapeake Bay weighed more than 65 pounds!*

## STATE CAT: CALICO

The Maryland legislature voted to adopt the calico cat as the state cat in 2001. Students from Westernport Elementary School in Allegany County came up with the idea and worked to have it approved. They noticed that the calico cat's colors—red, black, and white—are three of the four colors in the state flag.

*Maryland's state cat is the calico. "Calico" refers to the colors of a cat's fur, not to its breed.*

*The Baltimore checkerspot butterfly lives in wet meadows throughout Maryland. These butterflies cannot fly very fast or far, so it is easy to observe them.*

### STATE INSECT: CHECKERSPOT BUTTERFLY

The Maryland **Entomological** Society proposed that Maryland adopt an official insect, and in 1973 the Baltimore checkerspot butterfly joined the Maryland state symbols list. The Baltimore checkerspot has a dark brown body and brown wings spotted white and orange at the edges—the colors resemble Lord Baltimore's flag and gave the butterfly its name.

*The Chesapeake Bay Retriever has large, webbed feet and a unique, water-repelling coat.*

### STATE DOG: CHESAPEAKE BAY RETRIEVER

The Chesapeake Bay retriever became Maryland's state dog in 1964. The breed, one of only a few developed in the United States, probably came from two Newfoundland dogs who lived on opposite sides of the bay in the early 1800s.

### STATE CRUSTACEAN: BLUE CRAB

The blue crab had long been an unofficial symbol of Maryland when the legislature chose to make it the state **crustacean** in 1989. The business of catching and processing crabs brings hundreds of millions of dollars to the state each year. The bluish green crabs, which turn bright red when cooked, also provide Maryland's most famous foods: steamed crabs and crab cakes.

*People can tell male and female crabs apart by looking on the bottom of their shells. A male has markings that look a little like the Washington Monument, and an adult female has markings that look more like the U.S. Capitol dome.*

*This turtle takes its name from the diamond-shaped rings on its back. At the University of Maryland, they warn the teams they play to "Fear the turtle!"*

## STATE REPTILE: DIAMONDBACK TERRAPIN

Native Americans taught the European settlers to roast and eat the diamondback terrapin, a kind of turtle common in Maryland waters. The University of Maryland made the terrapin its mascot in 1933, and in 1994 the General Assembly chose the diamondback terrapin as Maryland's state reptile.

## STATE SPORT: JOUSTING

Jousting—a very unusual competition—became Maryland's state sport in 1962. Marylanders have been jousting for hundreds of years. The sport grew out of games knights played to practice their skills. In today's contests, people ride horses along a course where rings of a small diameter—less than two inches—hang overhead. The object is to spear these rings with a long-tipped lance while going as fast as possible.

*People who ride in jousting tournaments take a special name to go with the sport. For example, a man who lives in Island Creek might call himself "the Knight of Island Creek."*

## MARYLAND STATE QUARTER

Released in 2000, Maryland's state quarter shows the dome of the statehouse in Annapolis. Oak clusters, branches of Maryland's official state tree, and the state nickname, "The Old Line State," surround the dome's image. The statehouse appears on the quarter because so much Maryland—and some national—history happened there. It is the oldest statehouse in the United States still in use by the legislature.

*Maryland's dome is the largest wooden dome built without nails in the United States.*

# Maryland's History and People

The first humans came to present-day Maryland about 12,000 years ago. Historians know little about the earliest groups, who left behind nothing but the tips of their weapons.

## NATIVE AMERICANS

By the time European settlers arrived in the early 1600s, Native Americans had been building permanent villages in the region for several hundred years. Most of those living in the area spoke the Algonquin language. The Nanticoke, Choptank, Pocomoke, and others lived on the eastern side of the Chesapeake Bay. The Patuxent, Piscataway, Yaocomico, and others lived on the western side.

The Native Americans taught the settlers how to grow and cook crops unknown in Europe, such as corn,

*The Native Americans of Maryland were the first farmers to plant and grow pumpkin seeds. They used tools made of stone, animal bone, and tortoise shell to grow autumn vegatables, like the pumpkin, in the cold ground.*

squash, and pumpkins. They also gave them advice on clearing land, gathering oysters, hunting and fishing, and sailing the Chesapeake Bay.

## EXPLORATION AND SETTLEMENT

In 1608 Captain John Smith, an Englishman from the Jamestown, Virginia, settlement, made the first thorough exploration of the Chesapeake Bay by a European. Smith thought the area a fine location for more English settlements. Two decades later, the Calvert family took Smith's advice and began to settle the area.

George Calvert (1580–1632), the first Lord Baltimore, worked as a close adviser to King Charles I. At that time, the English government **persecuted** those who did not believe in the official state religion. When Calvert left the Church of England and became a Roman **Catholic** in 1625, his political career ended. He decided to look in a new direction, and he asked the king for a land grant in America. King Charles agreed. The grant became official two months after George Calvert died, so his oldest son Cecil (1605–1675), the second Lord Baltimore, received it.

## St. Mary's City— The First Settlement

Lord Baltimore's settlers were successful in their new home. St. Mary's City became the fourth permanent English settlement in North America and was the capital of Maryland from 1634 to 1694. All the original buildings from St. Mary's City have been gone for many years. Today, copies of the old buildings are part of a museum that teaches about Maryland in the 1600s.

Cecil, his brother Leonard, and a group of settlers crossed the Atlantic Ocean, sailed up the Chesapeake Bay to the Potomac River, and landed on St. Clement's Island. There Leonard Calvert solemnly read the land grant. Marylanders now remember that date, March 25, as Maryland Day.

The Calvert family's experience as Catholics in England taught them the importance of religious **tolerance.** They wanted the settlers in Maryland to be free to worship as they chose. In 1649 the local Toleration Act was enacted to protect both Catholics and **Protestants.** When the law passed, many people saw Maryland as a place unique among the colonies, a place of religious tolerance.

## AMERICAN REVOLUTION AND STATEHOOD

The **Revolutionary War** (1775–1783) ended British rule over the American colonies. No major battles took place in Maryland, but the colony supplied soldiers, weapons, and ships to the American army. In 1783 the **Continental Congress** met at the statehouse in Annapolis to sign the Treaty of Paris, which formally ended the war.

At the 1786 Annapolis Convention, the Continental Congress decided to call a meeting to design a stronger system of central government. At the Constitutional

*When the Continental Congress convened in Annapolis from November 26, 1783 to August 13, 1784, it met in the Old Senate Chamber of the Maryland Statehouse.*

## "The Star-Spangled Banner"

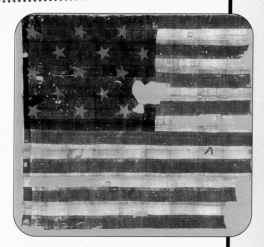

During the War of 1812, British forces attacked Baltimore by **bombarding** Fort McHenry. Francis Scott Key watched the nighttime battle through a spyglass from a boat eight miles downriver. At dawn the next day, Key could see that the U.S. flag still flew above the fort. He expressed his happiness and pride in a poem that became our national anthem, "The Star-Spangled Banner." The flag has been cared for by the Smithsonian Institution in Washington, D.C., since 1912.

Convention, held in Philadelphia in 1787, Maryland fought for the rights of smaller states. The makeup of the U.S. Senate, in which every state has two members no matter the population, was the result.

 Once the Constitution was written, Marylanders debated whether the state should ratify, or officially approve, the document. On April 28, 1788, Maryland's leaders voted to ratify the U.S. Constitution, and Maryland became the seventh state.

## FORT MCHENRY AND THE WAR OF 1812

In the early 1800s, war between France and England began to affect U.S. shipping, as each European country tried to prevent trade with the other. To protect its sailors and trade, the United States declared war on England in 1812. During the war, more than 100 privately owned armed ships sailed from Baltimore. These sleek, swift ships, known as Baltimore clippers, seized more than 550 British merchant ships. Their success at capturing English property made Baltimore a target for attack.

Baltimore's defense depended on Fort McHenry, a star-shaped fort surrounded by water on three sides. Ships had to pass by the fort in order to reach the city. Beginning early on September 13, 1814, British warships bombed Fort McHenry. The fort's guns answered the attack, and the British ships eventually withdrew. Their defeat at the Battle of Baltimore helped convince the British to end the war.

## THE CIVIL WAR

During the mid-1800s, Maryland's economy boomed. But the state seemed divided into two regions. Marylanders in the northern and western counties prospered through trade and manufacturing. But those in the southern counties and on the Eastern Shore tended to hold huge farms, which required low-cost labor to make a profit. Financial success depended on slavery, a cruel practice in which one person was considered the property of another.

People in the northern states opposed slavery, saying that it could not be accepted anywhere in the United States, a country founded on the principles of freedom. The southern states, whose economy depended on slavery, resisted any change. By 1861 the two sides were at war.

During the **Civil War** (1861–1865), Marylanders generally took sides according to region. Those from the western and northern counties fought for the **Union,** and those from the southern counties and lower Eastern Shore fought for the **Confederacy.** To make sure that Maryland would not join the Confederacy, President Abraham Lincoln sent Union troops to occupy Baltimore and Annapolis.

One of the most important Civil War battles took place in Maryland. In September 1862 Confederate and Union

# The Battle at Antietam Creek

On September 17, 1862, Union and Confederate soldiers fought a terrible battle behind Antietam Creek in Sharpsburg, Maryland. By day's end, more than 23,000 Americans had been killed or wounded. At one point, the soldiers fought on a low-lying road near the creek. So much blood fell

to the ground so quickly that it formed a stream. Witnesses named it Bloody Lane. The Antietam National Battlefield became a national park in 1890. Today, visitors to the park find peaceful, green fields where a historic battle once raged. The battle at Antietam Creek was the bloodiest day in American history.

soldiers met at Antietam Creek in western Maryland. It was one of the bloodiest battles of the war. The Union victory helped convince President Lincoln to issue the **Emancipation Proclamation.** However, when Lincoln issued the Emancipation Proclamation in 1862, he freed only slaves in Confederate states—not Maryland. Then in 1864, the Maryland legislature wrote a new state constitution that abolished slavery. They did so long before the **Thirteenth Amendment** to the U.S. Constitution went into effect in 1865.

## FAMOUS PEOPLE FROM MARYLAND

**Benjamin Banneker** (1731–1806), scientist. Born near Baltimore to an enslaved father and free mother, Banneker was free himself and able to attend school for a few years. He taught himself astronomy and advanced mathematics. Banneker helped Pierre L'Enfant lay out the site of Washington, D.C., and finished the project after L'Enfant left. By the time of his death, Banneker was a world-famous astronomer, author, and social critic.

**Roger B. Taney** (1777–1864), judge. Born into a wealthy family of southern Maryland tobacco farmers, Roger B. Taney practiced law and participated in Maryland state politics. In 1836 he was appointed Chief Justice of the United States Supreme Court. His most famous opinion came in *Dred Scott v. Sandford* (1857), in which he said that slaves could not become free by going to a free state; that slaves had no right to sue the federal government because they were not citizens; and that Congress could not prevent the territories from allowing slavery. Taney died before Congress ended slavery in all states in 1865.

**Edgar Allan Poe** (1809–1849), author. Edgar Allan Poe wrote poetry and the first stories known as mysteries. He started writing mysteries in Baltimore in the early 1830s. Later he moved to New York City, but he was passing through Baltimore when he died at age 40. Poe's fame and popularity have lasted much longer than his life. Baltimore's professional football team, the Ravens, took its name from "The Raven," one of Poe's poems.

*Every year since 1949, on Poe's birthday, a hooded figure leaves roses and a bottle of cognac on his grave in Baltimore. The visitor's identity? A mystery!*

**Frederick Douglass** (1817–1895), **abolitionist.** Born enslaved, Douglass became a household servant at age nine and learned to read. He escaped slavery as a young man, traveled northward, and worked for the Massachusetts Anti-Slavery Society. His impressive speeches made him a famous abolitionist. Later, Douglass founded and edited a newspaper, *The North Star.*

**Harriet Tubman** (1820–1913), conductor for the **Underground Railroad.** Harriet Tubman was born into slavery around 1820 near Cambridge on the Eastern Shore of Maryland. In 1849 she

escaped and ran northward, but she soon returned to help others escape, too. People fleeing slavery were described as passengers traveling on the Underground Railroad. Safe hiding places along the way were called stations, and those who guided the escaping slaves were called conductors.

**Babe Ruth** (1895–1948), baseball player. Born in Baltimore, Babe Ruth grew up in an **orphanage** and fell in love with baseball while playing at St. Mary's Industrial School for Boys. At age nineteen Ruth signed his first professional baseball contract with the Baltimore Orioles. He got his nickname when he appeared with Jack Dunn, a man known for signing young players, and someone remarked, "Well, here's Jack's newest babe." Ruth held 53 baseball records, including two of the most famous—60 home runs in a season, which lasted 34 years, and 714 career home runs, which lasted 39 years.

*Harriet Tubman became known as the Moses of her people because she led so many slaves to freedom, just as the biblical hero did. Between 1850 and 1860, Tubman led more than 300 slaves to freedom.*

**Thurgood Marshall** (1908–1993), Supreme Court justice. Born in Baltimore, Marshall played an important role in the history of civil rights in the United States. As chief counsel for the National Association for the Advancement of Colored People (NAACP), he argued and won the groundbreaking case of *Brown v. Board of Education* in 1954, which ended school **segregation.** In 1967 Marshall became the first African American justice on the United States Supreme Court.

*Before Babe Ruth became baseball's first great home run hitter, he pitched for the Boston Red Sox. He had a record of 23–12 in 1926 and 24–13 in 1917.*

# The Chesapeake Bay

**O**n a map of Maryland, the big, branching, blue area that nearly cuts the state in two is the Chesapeake Bay. The bay has influenced Maryland's history more than any other natural feature. In the 1600s the earliest European settlers followed the bay to find their new home, and seafood from the bay helped them survive once they got there. Since then, many Marylanders have earned their livings working on the bay, harvesting shellfish and fish. Others turn to the bay when they want to relax.

## Bay Basics

The Chesapeake Bay formed millions of years ago, as the last **Ice Age** ended. Melting glaciers raised sea levels, and ocean waters flooded the valley on either side of the ancient Susquehanna River. Today, the bay stretches 200 miles from the mouth of the Susquehanna to the Atlantic Ocean. The bay averages 21 feet deep, but a few channels of 100 feet or more allow ocean-going ships to pass.

*The Chesapeake shoreline is low, irregular, and often swampy.*

Maryland shares the bay with its neighbor Virginia, which owns the part closest to the ocean. In Maryland alone, the bay covers nearly 2,000 square miles and laps against more than 4,000 miles of winding shoreline.

*The mixture of saltwater and freshwater lets the bay support more than 3,600 species of plants and animals, including these crabs.*

The Chesapeake Bay is North America's largest **estuary.** About 50 major rivers flow into the Chesapeake. The biggest, the Susquehanna, pours in more than eighteen million gallons of freshwater per minute.

## GREAT SHELLFISH BAY

The Chesapeake Bay's name came from Native American words for "great shellfish bay." The name makes sense. Shellfish, such as oysters and crabs, and fish, such as rockfish and perch, thrive in the bay. The bay's shallow, traylike shape keeps the water warm, and its countless small coves offer fish and crabs safe feeding grounds.

## SAVING THE BAY

Close to twenty million people live in the area, called the Chesapeake Bay **watershed.** As a result, by the mid-1900s, people began to notice changes in the bay's water quality. As more people and more industry moved into the watershed, waste products had begun to change the bay. In the 1970s, Congress banned the use of certain **pesticides** and toxic chemicals. In 1983 a joint effort to restore the bay's health brought together Maryland, Pennsylvania, Virginia, Washington, D.C., the U.S. Environmental Protection Agency, and the Chesapeake Bay Commission. This partnership, called the Chesapeake Bay Program, now directs and manages the cleanup.

# Maryland's State Government

**T**he Maryland state government is much like the U.S. government. There are three main parts: the legislative branch, the executive branch, and the judicial branch. The government is based in Annapolis, the state capital.

## LEGISLATIVE BRANCH

In Maryland, the legislative branch of government is called the General Assembly. The 47-member senate and the 141-member house of delegates form the General Assembly. These two groups work together to make the state's laws. Maryland voters elect senators and delegates to four-year terms.

Each year, the General Assembly meets in the Maryland statehouse for a 90-day session. During that time, senators and delegates present and discuss bills, or ideas for new laws, and then vote to accept or reject them. Bills approved by both the senate and the house of delegates

*Maryland government leaders have been meeting in Annapolis since 1695.*

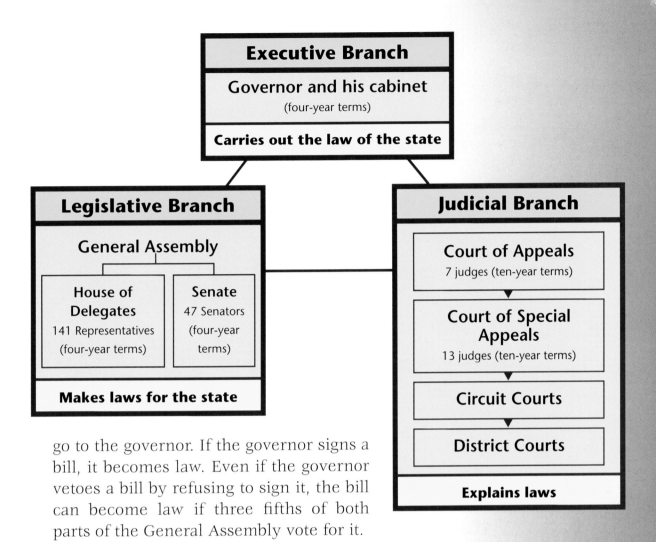

**Executive Branch**

**Governor and his cabinet**
(four-year terms)

**Carries out the law of the state**

**Legislative Branch**

**General Assembly**

| House of Delegates | Senate |
|---|---|
| 141 Representatives (four-year terms) | 47 Senators (four-year terms) |

**Makes laws for the state**

**Judicial Branch**

**Court of Appeals**
7 judges (ten-year terms)

**Court of Special Appeals**
13 judges (ten-year terms)

**Circuit Courts**

**District Courts**

**Explains laws**

go to the governor. If the governor signs a bill, it becomes law. Even if the governor vetoes a bill by refusing to sign it, the bill can become law if three fifths of both parts of the General Assembly vote for it.

## EXECUTIVE BRANCH

The governor heads the executive branch, which oversees the state government's day-to-day responsibilities. Elected by the voters to a four-year term, the governor runs the state with help from a group known as the cabinet. The cabinet includes the lieutenant governor and others who lead government departments. The governor may not serve more than two terms in a row.

## JUDICIAL BRANCH

The judicial branch of Maryland's government is the state court system. The court system interprets state law and figures out how laws apply to legal problems. The judicial branch has four levels: the district court, the circuit courts, the court of special appeals, and the court of appeals.

*For nine months in 1783–1784, the national government met in the Maryland statehouse. Here George Washington turned his sword over to Congress. This meant he was no longer the leader of the army.*

The District Court is the lowest, or least powerful, level in Maryland's court system. It handles minor **civil** and **criminal** cases, as well as all cases about motor vehicle laws. Appointed by the governor and confirmed by the Senate, district court judges serve ten-year terms.

The circuit courts, the level above the district court, have judges appointed by the governor and then approved by the voters. These judges each serve fifteen-year terms. The circuit courts hold jury trials and hear major civil cases, such as lawsuits involving more than $10,000, serious criminal cases, such as murder, and cases appealed from the district court.

Maryland's second highest court is the court of special appeals created in 1966. This court includes a chief judge and twelve other judges. Special appeals judges serve ten-year terms and hear cases that a lower court already decided. Someone unhappy with the first decision can ask for a review, or call an appeal, of the judgment.

The court of appeals is Maryland's highest court. The chief judge, who heads the state's court system, and six other judges sit on this court. After being appointed by the governor and confirmed by the Senate, these judges are elected by the voters each to ten-year terms. The court of appeals hears the most important appeals cases from the lower courts, either directly or after the court of special appeals has ruled. The Maryland court of appeals judges are the only ones in the United States to wear red robes, a tradition from colonial times.

# Maryland's Culture

The people of Maryland have developed a state culture that is unique. Where else can you find stately **colonial** mansions, contests in crab racing and oyster shucking, the Kunta Kinte festival, and painted window screens? Nowhere but in Maryland!

## COLONIAL INFLUENCES

Marylanders have worked hard to preserve their colonial heritage. They built a copy of the 1634 settlement at St. Mary's City. There, visitors can see what life was like for the settlers. Museum guides dress in the clothes of the 1600s and do everyday activities, such as playing the board games popular at that time. They also act out historical scenes, such as trials based on court records. Visitors tour the areas where scientists continue to dig, searching for more clues to the past. Several special events draw crowds every year. Tidewater **Archaeology** Weekend offers visitors the chance to join the scientists in the field and help sift the dirt for new finds. And Maryland Day centers around a full-size copy of the *Dove,* one of the two ships that carried the settlers across the Atlantic Ocean.

One of the best-preserved colonial cities in the country is Annapolis. Maryland's government moved from St. Mary's City to Annapolis in 1695. As state government workers walk its shaded streets, they pass more buildings from the 1700s than can be found anywhere else in the country.

## THE MARYLAND WATERMAN

Each year, two special events highlight the work of Maryland's watermen, the people who earn money by fishing, crabbing, and oystering in the Chesapeake Bay.

# The U.S. Naval Academy

Visitors to Annapolis see many young people around town wearing snappy white uniforms. They are students at the U.S. Naval Academy, a college for future officers of the U.S. Navy and Marine Corps. Opened in 1845, the Naval Academy educates its students, called midshipmen, for free, and the

midshipmen agree to serve in the navy or marines for at least five years after graduation. Graduates include former president Jimmy Carter and at least 50 astronauts. In 1976 the first female students entered the Naval Academy. Today, women make up about fifteen percent of the school.

In September, Crisfield holds the National Hard Crab Derby and Fair. People come to watch the race and the beauty pageant—crowning Miss **Crustacean**—see fireworks, and eat spicy steamed crabs.

The National Oyster Shucking Contest takes place in October at the St. Mary's County Oyster Festival. To shuck an oyster, the shell must be opened and the oyster inside detached. People in the contest must shuck quickly and skillfully. The winner goes to the world championships in Ireland.

## AFRICAN AMERICANS

Africans came to the shores of the Chesapeake with the early English settlers. Some, but not all, were enslaved. By 1850 about 25,000 free African Americans lived in Baltimore, more than in any other city in the country.

Today, about 28 percent of the people in Maryland are African American. Recently, Prince George's County, fifteen miles west of Annapolis in southern Maryland, has become known as the wealthiest county in the United States in which most of the people are African American.

Each summer, many African Americans in Maryland attend the Kunta Kinte Heritage Festival. In his famous book *Roots,* Alex Haley describes his ancestor Kunta Kinte's arrival in Annapolis as a slave in 1767. The festival remembers Kunta Kinte's life. People can listen to the tales of griots, or storytellers, just as Alex Haley listened to his grandmother tell the story of his family.

## Painted Window Screens

Baltimore has a unique artistic tradition—the painted window screen. In 1913 William Oktavec painted a colorful picture on his screens to shade the fruit and vegetables he was selling inside. Oktavec's idea spread. By the 1930s, 100,000 painted door and window screens decorated Baltimore. Painted screens fell out of fashion after air conditioning came along. Fewer than 3,000 remain today.

# Maryland's Food

**M**arylanders love to eat. And why not? The Chesapeake Bay serves up delicious crabs, rockfish, and oysters. The farms of the Eastern Shore grow sweet corn and tomatoes that complement any dish. Dessert might be sliced watermelon or eight-layer cakes.

## CRAB HAPPY

Crabs are Maryland's most famous food. People make crab cakes—much like hamburgers, but with crabmeat—crab soup, and crab imperial, a fancy hot dish made with mayonnaise. At a traditional Maryland crab feast, friends and family relax around long tables covered with

## Crab Talk

The way that Maryland watermen talk about crabs is unique. Now you can learn what it means when you hear, "Look at that jimmy go! He must be chasing that sook over there."

| | |
|---|---|
| **jimmy** | an adult male crab |
| **sook** | an adult female crab |
| **sally** | a young female crab |
| **doubler** | a pair of crabs, male and female, moving as one |
| **peeler** | crab that will soon shed its hard shell |
| **buster** | crab that has started shedding |
| **softshell** | crab that has finished shedding |

# Maryland Crab Cakes

1 egg

¼ cup mayonnaise

1 teaspoon Old Bay (or other seafood seasoning)

¼ teaspoon white pepper

2 teaspoons Worcestershire sauce

1 teaspoon dry mustard

1 pound Maryland crabmeat (fresh)

½ cup cracker crumbs or bread crumbs

**Ask an adult to help you when it is time to cook the crab cakes!**

Gently feel through the crabmeat to find and remove any pieces of shell. In a bowl, mix together egg, mayonnaise, seafood seasoning, white pepper, Worcestershire sauce, and dry mustard. Add crabmeat; mix carefully. Stir in cracker crumbs. Shape into six cakes. Have an adult help you deep-fry the crab cakes in oil at 350° F for two to three minutes, until golden brown. Or sauté them in a frying pan with a little oil for five minutes on each side. The crab cakes taste good in a sandwich or on their own.

newspaper. Rolls of paper towels are nearby because this is a messy meal!

## THE SOFTER SIDE OF CRABS

A blue crab sheds its hard outer shell about twenty times during its three years of life. Each time it sheds, the crab grows about one third bigger. For a few hours, just after shedding, the crab has a soft shell. Before the shell hardens again, a soft crab can be cleaned, cooked, and eaten whole.

# Maryland's Folklore and Legends

**F**olklore is a set of sayings and stories that are unique to a certain place or group of people. Handed down through the generations, folklore often explains why things are a certain way. These stories can be educational and fun, but they are rarely true. A legend is a popular story, sometimes based on real events. Both folktales and legends are meant to entertain.

### CHESSIE

Tales of giant sea serpents, or snakes, surface in many places. Scotland's Loch Ness monster, nicknamed Nessie, may be the most famous. Maryland has a sea serpent, too, called Chessie. For more than twenty years, people have reported seeing a huge, snakelike animal in the Chesapeake Bay. They usually described a playful,

greenish-brown reptile about 30 feet long. In 1982, scientists at the Smithsonian Institution studied a videotape of a Chessie sighting. They said that the creature taped was alive, but they could not tell exactly what it was.

The legend of Chessie the sea serpent may be based on sightings of a large marine mammal called a manatee. In 1994 a manatee showed up in the Chesapeake Bay, hundreds of miles from its Florida home. Scientists caught and tagged it for identification, then flew it back to Florida. The manatee, which also came to be called Chessie, returned to the bay less than a year later. It seems to swim up and down the coast on a regular basis. The most recent sighting of Chessie the manatee was in Virginia in 2001. The last time anyone reported seeing Chessie the sea serpent was in 1995.

## BARBARA FRIETCHIE

Legend tells of a Maryland patriot who became famous during the **Civil War.** Her name was Barbara Frietchie. In 1862 at age 95, she boldly hung the Union flag from her window as Confederate soldiers passed by her home in Frederick. In tribute to her bravery, the soldiers did not harm her. When the poet John Greenleaf Whittier heard her story, he wrote a poem about her bravery. Here is the most famous part of it: "'Shoot, if you must, this old gray head, / But spare your country's flag,' she said."

*Barbara Frietchie was born in Lancaster. She is buried in the graveyard of the German Reformed Church in Frederick.*

# Maryland's Sports Teams

**M**arylanders enjoy watching college and professional sports teams play, and in recent years, fans have cheered several national champions.

## PROFESSIONAL SPORTS

Baltimore is crazy about its baseball team. The Orioles have played major league baseball in Baltimore since 1954. They won the World Series in 1966, 1970, and 1983. The team plays in downtown Baltimore in Oriole Park at Camden Yards. The ballpark, open since 1992, sits two blocks from the birthplace of Babe Ruth.

The Baltimore Ravens became the city's professional football team in 1996. The Ravens defense set a record for points allowed in an NFL season and helped them win the Super Bowl in 2001. They play in a new stadium near the Orioles' home in downtown Baltimore.

*Part of the Camden Yards complex is the Baltimore and Ohio Warehouse, located just behind right field. At 1,016 feet in length, it is the longest building on the East Coast.*

# Maryland Horseracing

Maryland holds two famous races each year. The Preakness Stakes is the second jewel in the **Triple Crown.** It is run after the Kentucky Derby and before the Belmont Stakes. The Preakness takes place on the third Saturday of May at Baltimore's Pimlico Race Course. The Maryland Hunt Cup Race, first held in 1894, is the country's oldest and longest steeplechase, a race that includes jumps over wooden rails and water. In late April, fans gather on a hill north of Baltimore that overlooks the racecourse. Because the horses must combine running at great speed with jumping, steeplechase racing is one of the most dangerous sports.

## COLLEGE SPORTS

The University of Maryland fields teams in a variety of sports. Since 1953 the school has won 21 national championships in a variety of sports. The men's basketball team has played well for decades and finally won its first national championship in 2002. The women's lacrosse team has won nine national championships, including seven straight from 1995 to 2001, and the field hockey team has won four national championships. Another Maryland school, Johns Hopkins University, has won seven national championships in men's lacrosse, more than any other school.

*Lacrosse has been popular in Maryland since the late 1800s.*

# Maryland's Businesses and Products

**M**aryland's most famous product is the blue crab, but many other businesses contribute to the state's healthy **economy.**

## INDUSTRY

Maryland businesses produce food items, chemicals, computer and electronic products, machinery, transportation equipment, lumber, and printed products, such as magazines and newspapers. Large companies based in Maryland include McCormick and Black and Decker. McCormick has been operating since 1889, when Willoughby McCormick sold root beer and fruit syrups out of his one-room house in Baltimore. McCormick is now the world's largest spice maker. Black and Decker has been around since 1917, when S. Duncan Black and Alonzo Decker developed the first portable drill. Today, Black and Decker is a $5 billion global corporation.

. . . . . . . . . . . . . . . . . . . . . . . . . . .

*On September 2, 1889, Willoughby McCormick and his staff of two girls and a boy began operating at McCormick and Company.*

Maryland's seafood industry adds about $400 million to the state's economy each year. The fish and shellfish taken from the bay include rockfish, oysters, soft clams, flounder, perch, spot, croakers, catfish, sea trout, and bluefish. But the blue crab stands alone as Maryland's most valuable catch. The Chesapeake Bay supplies 50 percent of the total blue crab harvest in the United States.

## FARM PRODUCTS

Agriculture, or farming, takes up about one third of Maryland's land and employs more than 350,000 people. Most farms are in the central part of the state and on the upper Eastern Shore. Chicken farming on the Eastern Shore brings in about one third of the total money from agriculture. Other important farm products include both greenhouse and nursery plants, and milk and dairy products.

## TOURISM

Maryland draws nearly 20 million visitors each year, making tourism an $8 billion industry for the state. Many tourists visit Baltimore, which claims to have more museums per person than any other U.S. city. While there, they head to the Inner Harbor, an area that used to be an unappealing, run-down part of the city. Then, in 1980 the Harborplace buildings opened, and the crowds have come ever since to shop, eat, and enjoy the view.

*Water taxis carry people between spots in the Inner Harbor, Baltimore's most popular destination. It was full of decaying wharfs and warehouses only 25 years ago.*

# Attractions and Landmarks

**M**aryland's long history has made it a great place to visit. For such a small state, there certainly is much to see and do!

### ANNAPOLIS

Shipping brought great wealth to colonial Annapolis, and in the 1700s people built mansions as nice as those in England. Walking tours of the winding, brick-paved streets in the historic district are popular, and the statehouse draws many visitors.

### BALTIMORE

Visitors to Baltimore see many historic sites and museums. At the Inner Harbor, people can tour the U.S. Navy's last ship powered only by sails, the 1854 U.S.S. *Constellation*. They also can visit the seven-story National Aquarium, Maryland's biggest paid tourist attraction.

*Tourists often visit the beautiful 1760 house and garden of William Paca, who signed the Declaration of Independence.*

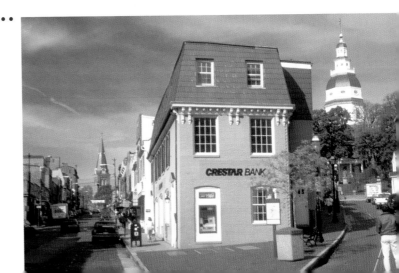

*This exhibit from the Great Blacks in Wax Museum shows great African-American educators—George Washington Carver, Booker T. Washington, and Mary McLeod Bethune.*

More than 10,000 creatures live in the aquarium's million gallons of water and roof-top rain forest.

About three miles north of the Inner Harbor is the Great Blacks in Wax Museum. This first-and-only wax museum of African American history presents more than 100 lifelike wax figures of people from ancient Africa to the present. It also displays a copy of the type of ship used to carry slaves from Africa to the United States.

## Places to see in Maryland

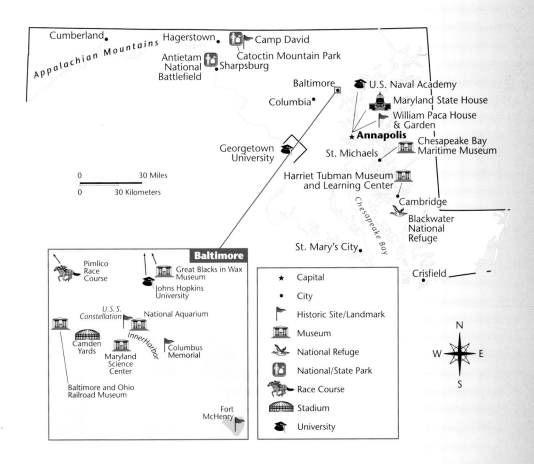

*At the Chesapeake Bay Maritime Museum, visitors can try using the tools of the waterman, including dip nets, trotlines, crab pots, and oyster tongs.*

## EASTERN SHORE STOP

On the Eastern Shore is the Chesapeake Bay Maritime Museum in St. Michaels, founded in 1965. It tells the story of the bay, Maryland's watermen, the boats they have used, and the seafood they have caught. Children can board and explore a miniature skipjack, one of Maryland's unique sailing workboats, or tour a lighthouse and learn about what a lighthouse keeper does. Watermen, decoy carvers, crab pickers, and boat builders come to the museum to tell visitors about their special skills.

## WESTERN SHORE SPOT

Camp David is a presidential retreat deep within western Maryland's Catoctin Mountain Park. The camp, named after President Dwight Eisenhower's (1890–1969) grandson David, has been a presidential hideaway since the 1930s. Sometimes the president meets with national and world leaders at Camp David, and important documents have been signed there. For example, in 1978 President Carter met there with the leaders of Israel and Egypt, who agreed to the historic peace settlement known as the Camp David Accords. Tourists cannot visit Camp David, but they can hike the park's trails and enjoy the same peaceful beauty that the president admires.

# Map of Maryland

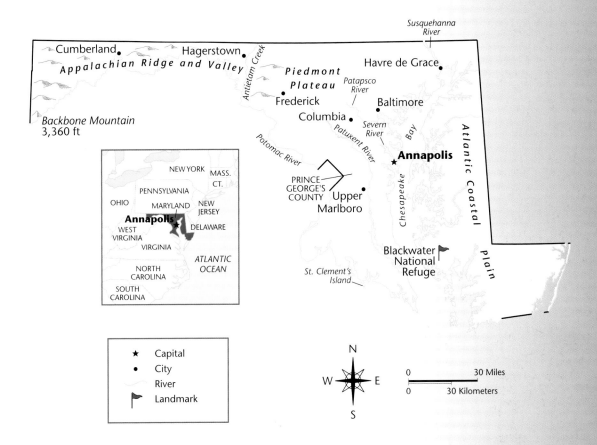

Susquehanna River

Cumberland
Hagerstown
Appalachian Ridge and Valley
Antietam Creek
Piedmont Plateau
Havre de Grace
Patapsco River
Frederick
Baltimore
Backbone Mountain
3,360 ft
Columbia
Severn River
Potomac River
Patuxent River
**Annapolis**
Chesapeake Bay
Atlantic Coastal
PRINCE GEORGE'S COUNTY
Upper Marlboro
Blackwater National Refuge
plain
St. Clement's Island

NEW YORK
MASS.
CT.
PENNSYLVANIA
OHIO
MARYLAND
NEW JERSEY
**Annapolis**
WEST VIRGINIA
DELAWARE
VIRGINIA
ATLANTIC OCEAN
NORTH CAROLINA
SOUTH CAROLINA

★ Capital
• City
～ River
⚑ Landmark

N
W E
S

| 0 | 30 Miles |
| 0 | 30 Kilometers |

# Glossary

**abolitionist** member of the social movement before the Civil War (1861–1865) that demanded an end to slavery

**agricultural** relating to the science of cultivating the soil, producing crops, and raising livestock

**archaeology** the study of objects from the past, including pottery, fossils, and other artifacts

**bishop** a clergyman ranked above a priest, who has the power to ordain and confirm and is in charge of a church district

**bombarding** attacking forcefully or continuously with bombs or heavy gunfire

**Catholic** a member of the Christian church headed by the Pope

**civil** relating to court action between individuals having to do with private rights rather than criminal action

**Civil War** (1861–1865) the war in the United States between the Union and the Confederacy

**coats of arms** a shield that indicates peoples' ancestors and heritage

**colonial** being a part of a colony, which is land ruled by a foreign country

**Confederacy** the eleven southern states that seceded (withdrew) from the United States during the Civil War (1861–1865)

**Continental Congress** from 1774–1789 the federal legislature of the thirteen colonies and later of the United States

**criminal** dealing with a crime and its punishment

**crustacean** belonging to a class of animals that live in water, breathe through gills, and have a hard outer shell, such as shrimp, crabs, and lobsters

**economy** a system that manages resources, such as money, material, or labor

**ecosystem** a system made up of an ecological community and its environment

**electromagnetic** relating to magnetism developed by a current of electricity

**Emancipation Proclamation** a historic document issued by Abraham Lincoln in 1863 that led to the end of slavery

**emboss** to decorate with a raised pattern or design

**endangered** threatened with extinction

**entomological** relating to branch of zoology that deals with insects

**estuary** place where the sea and a river meet

**habitat** the place where a plant or animal naturally grows or lives

**heraldic banner** a flag bearing a design that features a coat of arms, sometimes carried as a battle standard

**immigrant** person who comes to a country to live there

**insecticide** chemical used to kill insects

**Lord Baltimore** also known as Cecilius Calvert, he helped establish the colony of Maryland in 1635

**Mason–Dixon line** the boundary between Maryland and Pennsylvania, regarded as the division between the free and slave-holding states during the Civil War

**motto** a sentence, phrase, or word inscribed on something (as a coin or public building) to suggest its use or nature; a guiding rule of conduct

**orphanage** an institution for the care of parentless children

**persecute** to cause to suffer because of a belief

**pesticide** chemical used for killing insects and weeds

**planned communities** a community, designed by builders or cities, with a variety of new homes and buildings that include recreational facilities that members of the community share

**Protestant** a member of a Christian church other than Catholic

**Revolutionary War** (1775–1783) war that the thirteen colonies fought to gain independence from Great Britain

**segregation** the separation or isolation of a race, class, or group (as by restriction to an area or by separate schools)

**temperate** having weather conditions that are usually mild

**Thirteenth Amendment** the amendment to the U.S. Constitution that made slavery illegal

**tolerance** sympathy for or acceptance of feelings, habits, or beliefs that are different from one's own

**Triple Crown** horse racing title won by a three-year-old horse that wins the Kentucky Derby, the Preakness, and the Belmont Stakes

**Underground Railroad** a secret group that helped slaves escape from the South to the free states in the North

**Union** something (as a nation) formed by a combining of parts or members; the northern states during the U.S. Civil War (1861–1865)

**watershed** the land area drained by a river system or bay

# More Books to Read

· · · · · · · · · · · · · · · · · · · · · · · · · · · · · · · · · · · · · · ·

Johnston, Joyce. *Maryland.* Minneapolis, Minn.: Lerner Publishing Group, 2002.

Kummer, Patricia K., Joe A. Swisher, and Betty Sue Swisher. *Maryland (One Nation).* Mankato, Minn.: Capstone Press, 2002.

Martin, Michael A., and Jean Craven. *Maryland: The Old Line State.* Milwaukee, Wis.: Gareth Stevens Publishing, 2002.

Pell, Ed, and Cynthia Neverdon-Morton. *Maryland.* Mankato, Minn.: Capstone Press, 2003.

Wilson, Richard, and E.L. Brindner Jr. *Maryland: Its Past and Present.* Lanham, Md.: Maryland Historical Press, 1999.

# Index

# About the Authors

**Jennifer Leese** is a mother, author, copyeditor, and children's book review columnist who lives in Maryland. She has also published several children's fiction books, young adult novels, and paranormal romance novels for adults.

**Loleta Gwynn** is a writer and editor who lives in Chevy Chase, Maryland. She grew up in southern Maryland and still spends time there catching and eating crabs—her children's favorite Maryland tradition.